INCHES GELETA

Diese Buchreihe versammelt die Bauwerke einzelner, mit hohem Qualitätsanspruch ausgewählter jüngerer Schweizer Architekten. Seit 2004 kuratiere ich die Reihe *Anthologie* in der Form einfacher Werkdokumentationen. Sie ist vergleichbar mit der «Blütenlese», wie sie in der Literatur für eine Sammlung ausgewählter Texte angewendet wird. Es liegt in der Natur des Architektenberufs, dass die Erstlingswerke junger Architekten meist kleinere übersichtliche Bauaufgaben sind. Sie sind eine Art Fingerübung, mit der sie das Erlernte anwenden und ihr architektonisches Sensorium erproben und entfalten können. Die Begabung und die Leidenschaft für das Metier lassen sich dabei früh in voller Deutlichkeit und Frische erkennen. So stecken in jedem der kleinen und grossen Projekte inspirierte Grundgedanken und Vorstellungen, die spielerisch und gleichermassen perfekt in architektonische Bilder, Formen und Räume umgesetzt werden. Damit wird mir wieder einmal bewusst, dass in der Architektur wie in anderen Kunstformen die Bilder und Ideen, die hinter dem Werk stehen, das Wesentliche sind. Es mag diese Intuition sein, die der Künstler hat, und die dann über sein Werk wie ein Funke auf den Betrachter überspringt, so wie es der italienische Philosoph Benedetto Croce in seinen Schriften eindringlich beschreibt.

Heinz Wirz
Verleger

This book series presents buildings by selected young Swiss architects that set themselves high quality standards. Since 2004, i have been curating the *Anthologie* series by simply documenting their oeuvre. The series can be compared to a literary anthology presenting a collection of selected texts. It is in the nature of the architectural profession that early works by young architects are mostly small, limited building tasks. They are a kind of five-finger exercise in which the architects apply what they have learnt, as well as testing and developing their architectural instincts. Talent and a passion for the profession can be seen at an early stage in all of its clarity and freshness. Each project, be it large or small, contains an inspired underlying concept and ideas that are playfully and consummately implemented as architectural images, forms and spaces. Thus, I am regularly reminded that in architecture, as in other art forms, the images and ideas behind the works are their essence. Perhaps this is the same intuition described so vividly by the Italian philosopher Benedetto Croce, one that is absorbed by the artist and flies like a spark via the work to the viewer.

Heinz Wirz
Publisher

INCHES GELETA

QUART

HAUS RIZZA, VACALLO

Projekt 2010, Ausführung 2012

Haus Rizza befindet sich in der Altstadt von Vacallo, einer Gemeinde mit Sied lungen, die teilweise bis ins 19. Jahrhundert zurückreichen. Der ursprüngliche Bau ist ein «Turmhaus» mit vier Geschossen über einem quadratischen Grund riss von 6 × 6 Metern. Aufgrund von Beschränkungen durch örtliche Bauvor schriften blieb seine Hülle unverändert: Die Öffnungen sind die gleichen, ebensc die Höhe der Traufe und des Firsts sowie der Typ des Schrägdachs. Die tra genden Aussenmauern sind die einzigen bereits bestehenden Elemente, die unangetastet blieben. Wegen des teilweise instabilen Zustands von Wänder und Decken wurde das Innere komplett entkernt und gänzlich neu aufgebaut

RIZZA HOUSE, VACALLO

Project 2010, Construction 2012

Rizza house is located in the historical centre of Vacallo, a small towr with a portion of settlements dating back to the 19th century. The origina house is a "tower building" with a square 6 x 6 m ground plan and 4 level: Due to restrictions set by local building laws, the envelope has no changed: the apertures were preserved, as were the eaves height, the ridge and the type of pitched roof. The load-bearing exterior walls are the only pre-existing elements that remained untouched. The interior wa totally gutted, partly because of the precarious condition of the wall and floors, and completely rebuilt.

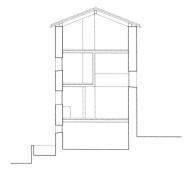

HAUS DESGRAZ, LOCARNO

Projekt 2011, Ausführung 2015

In der Altstadt von Solduno, einem Bezirk Locarnos, wurde ein Bestandsge
bäude modernisiert. Unter Einhaltung der Bauvorschriften eignet sich das
Projekt die für Tessiner *nuclei* typischen formalen Aspekte an und betont mit
dem Dachoberlicht gleichzeitig die charakteristischen Merkmale der histori
schen Aussenmauern. Das Innere ist ein Mikrokosmos, in dem die Materialität
von Böden- und Deckenbelägen zur räumlichen Definition beiträgt.

DESGRAZ HOUSE, LOCARNO

Project 2011, Construction 2015

An existing house was refurbished in the historical centre of Solduno, a
district of Locarno. In compliance with building regulations, the project
appropriates the formal aspects typical of Ticino's *nuclei* and at the same
time underlines the characteristics of the historical perimeter walls
thanks to the light crowning of the roof. The interior is a microcosm in
which the materiality of the floor and ceiling covering becomes a com
ponent of spatial definition.

MUSEUM MECRÌ, MINUSIO

Projekt 2012, Ausführung 2014

Beim Museum MeCrì handelt es sich um den Umbau eines ehemaligen Wohn hauses im historischen Ortskern von Minusio. Während die konstruktive Hülle unverändert blieb, wurde das Innere vollständig entkernt und neu ausgebaut - abgesehen von dem überwölbten Raum im Erdgeschoss, der an die ursprüngliche Funktion des Gebäudes erinnert. Die Ausstellungsräume bilden ein *continuum* und schaffen zwischen den einzelnen Ebenen neue räumliche Erfahrungen und Beziehungen. Eine leichte Metalltreppe verbindet sie miteinander. Die oberste Etage schliesst mit einer weissen Dachkonstruktion aus Holz ab.

MECRÌ MUSEUM, MINUSIO

Project 2012, Construction 2014

The MeCrì Museum is the transformation of an existing house in the his torical core of Minusio. While the structural envelope has not changed the interior has been totally emptied and completely rebuilt apart from the vaulted room on the ground floor, which is a reminder of the build ing's original function. The exhibition spaces are a *continuum*, creating new spatial experiences and relationships between each floor. A light weight metal staircase connects each level of the museum and the final floor is crowned by a white roof timber structure.

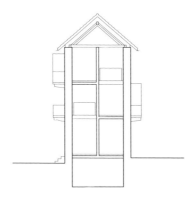

PAVILLON MECRÌ, MINUSIO
Projekt 2014, Ausführung 2016

Der Pavillon vermittelt zwischen den denkmalgeschützten Steinmauern de Grundstücksgrenzen und den Aussenwänden der Erweiterung durch seine Materialität und den Verweis auf ihre ursprüngliche Höhe und Länge. Wenn die alten Steinmauern im Laufe der Zeit verfallen, werden die neuen Wasch betonwände sichtbar. Die Wände des Erweiterungsbaus definieren einen Inner hof, der die beiden Teile des Museums MeCrì miteinander verbindet. Da monolithische Giebeldach über dem neuen Ausstellungsraum fügt sich mit se ner Form und den verwendeten Materialien in seine Umgebung ein. Im Innern des Pavillons erzeugt das Oberlicht auf dem Dach eine mystische Atmosphäre

MECRÌ PAVILION, MINUSIO
Project 2014, Construction 2016

The pavilion creates a dialogue between the protected stone walls sul rounding the site and those of the intervention through the materialit and by recalling their original height and length: as the old stone wall will degrade through time, the new washed concrete boundaries will stand in their place. The walls of the intervention define an inner courtyard conceived as a void that connects the two parts of the MeCrì Museun The monolithic pitched roof that covers the new exhibition room is inte grated into its surroundings, thanks to its form and use of material: The skylight crowning the top of the roof creates a mystic atmosphere in the inner space of the pavilion.

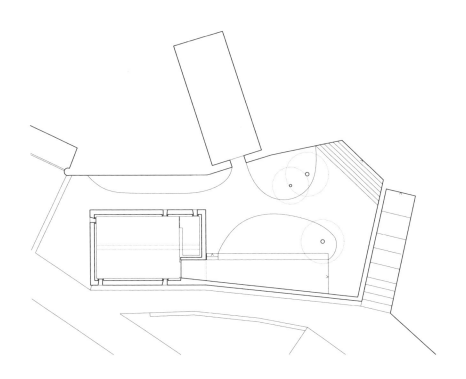

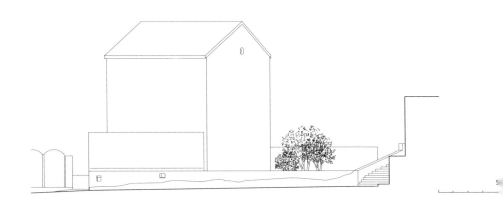

18

WOHNUNG SPEZIALI, LOCARNO
Projekt 2016, Ausführung 2017

Im Haus Canfora, einer Villa aus dem frühen 20. Jahrhundert mit Blick auf Locarno, wurde ein unbewohntes Dachgeschoss zu einer Wohnung umgebaut. Die tragenden Innen- und Aussenwände blieben aus konstruktiven Gründer unberührt, während die vorhandenen Trennwände, die das Dachgeschoss zer teilten, entfernt wurden. Die Arbeiten aus Holz wurden instand gesetzt und teilweise ersetzt, das Heizungssystem ausgetauscht. Sorgfältig ausgewählte Materialien, durchgebildete Türschwellen, Einbaumöbel und die Behandlung der Oberflächen kennzeichnen die Raumübergänge.

SPEZIALI APARTMENT, LOCARNO
Project 2016, Construction 2017

The intervention transforms an uninhabited attic space inside Canfora House, an early 20th-century villa overlooking the city of Locarno. The outer and inner load-bearing walls remained untouched for structura reasons while existing partitions that fragmented internal spaces were demolished. The wooden carpentry was renovated and partially replaced while the heating system was substituted. Inside, the transition between apartment spaces is signalled by the careful use of materials and the detailing of the thresholds, using fixed furnishings and the treatment of surfaces.

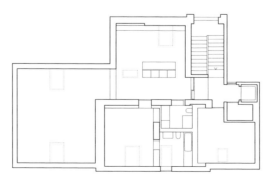

PALAZZO PIODA, LOCARNO
Projekt 2016, Ausführung 2018

Der Palazzo Pioda steht im Stadtteil Campagna, einem gemischt genutzten Viertel Locarnos. Die Parameter für die Baudichte sind hier höher als anderswo in der Stadt, was den Wunsch nach einer neuen Urbanität am Wohnort zum Ausdruck bringt. Das Volumen des Gebäudes bestimmten die Grenzabstände und die Bauvorschriften. Das sechsgeschossige Wohnhaus ist eine Hybridkonstruktion mit je einer Wohnung pro Stockwerk. Sein aussen liegendes Tragwerk bekundet Erhabenheit sowie städtische Integrität und prägt die Fassade. Dagegen betonen seine vorgefertigten Fassadenelemente aus Lochblech den halb industriellen und vom Handwerk geprägten Charakter des Viertels.

PALAZZO PIODA, LOCARNO
Project 2016, Construction 2018

The Palazzo Pioda stands in the Campagna district, a mixed-use neighbourhood of Locarno. The building density parameters are higher here than anywhere else in the city, which shows the desire to give the neighbourhood a new urbanity. Boundary distances and building laws determined the volume of the building. Extending over six storeys, the residential building is a hybrid construction that provides one apartment per floor. By turning the load-bearing structure outwards, on the one hand it shows its dignity and urban integrity, thus determining the façade, while on the other hand the prefabricated façade elements made of perforated sheet metal emphasise the semi-industrial and handcrafted character of the place.

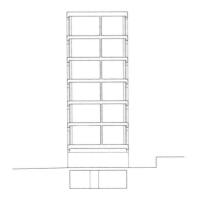

10

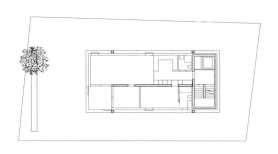

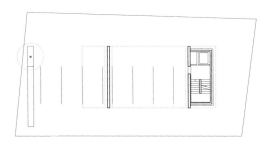

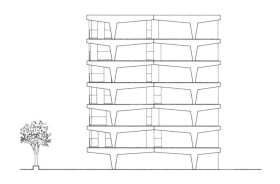

10

SCHULERWEITERUNG, VIGANELLO
Wettbewerb 2017, 1. Preis

Das Wettbewerbsprogramm beinhaltete eine Erweiterung der Grundschule in Viganello, um Platz für eine Kantine und einen ausserschulischen Freizeitraum für etwa 100 Kinder zu schaffen. Das Projekt ergänzt einen Entwurf des Architekten Sergio Pagnamenta von 1974 mit einem leichten Dachaufbau, der in Form und Materialien auf das bestehende Schulgebäude und auf die öffentlichen Bauten der Vergangenheit abgestimmt ist. Ein Stahltragwerk definiert die Gebäudefassade, indem sich Massstab, Gliederung und Farbe der bereits vorhandenen Elemente fortsetzen. Zu der Intervention gehören ein Dachgarten im Süden und ein geschützter Bereich im Westen, der sich an einen Raum für Freizeitaktivitäten anschliesst.

SCHOOL EXTENSION, VIGANELLO
Competition 2017, 1st Prize

The competition brief called for an extension of the Viganello elementary school to provide space for a canteen and an after-school activity room for around 100 children. The project amplifies a 1974 design by the architect Sergio Pagnamenta with a lightweight rooftop extension that is formally and materially integrated into the existing building and the expression of public architecture of the past. It uses a steel frame that defines the building's façade by continuing the scale, rhythm and colour of the pre-existing elements. The intervention features a rooftop garden to the south and a sheltered area to the west, adjacent to a room for extracurricular activities.

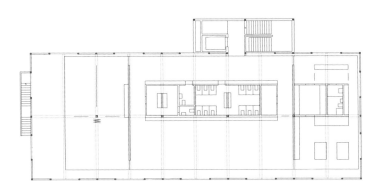

10

SCHULERWEITERUNG, MELANO
Wettbewerb 2018, 1. Preis

Form und Lage des Neubaus definieren und unterstreichen das Gebäudevolumen des Schulgebäudes. Ausserdem schaffen und kennzeichnen sie einen wichtigen Ort der Begegnung, den zentralen «Platz», sodass ungenutzte Aussenflächen vermieden werden. Die typologische Einfachheit sorgt für eine sehr flexible Trennung und Unterteilung der Klassenräume und ermöglicht künftig räumliche Veränderungen. Das transparente neue Volumen stellt einen Dialog zwischen den inneren Verkehrsflächen und den Aussenräumen her.

SCHOOL EXTENSION, MELANO
Competition 2018, 1st Prize

The form and position of the new building on the one hand defines and further enhances the volumetric conformation of the school sector and on the other generates and qualifies an important meeting place: the central "square", thus avoiding the creation of residual external spaces. The typological simplicity allows great flexibility in the separation and distribution of classrooms, offering the possibility of future spacial modifications. The transparency of the new volume creates a dialogue between the interior walkways and the exterior spaces.

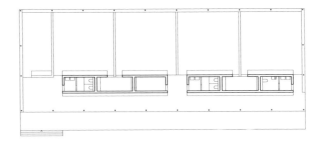

MASTERPLAN EX MACELLO – EX GAS, LOCARNO
Wettbewerb 2018, 1. Preis

Das fragliche Gebiet ist ein wesentlicher Bestandteil im städtischen Gefüge Locarnos. Es liegt unweit des Quartiere Nuovo, das Anfang des 20. Jahrhunderts mit neuen Achsen und Wohngebieten zur Umgestaltung der Stadt beitrug. Der Projektvorschlag sieht vor, das Areal von Ex Marcello – Ex Gas gänzlich in den übrigen Teil der Stadt zu integrieren. Dazu sollen die funktionalen und räumlichen Beziehungen zu den angrenzenden Grundstücken, den Nachbarhäusern und dem Sportzentrum ausgebaut werden. Mit einer neuen Identifikation und dem Gefühl der Zugehörigkeit zu diesem Ort sollen sich auch die Lebensbedingungen und das allgemeine Wohlbefinden der Bewohner verbessern.

MASTERPLAN EX MACELLO – EX GAS, LOCARNO
Competition 2018, 1st Prize

The area of concern is an important component of Locarno's urban fabric and is located near the New Quarter, which helped redesign the urban fabric of the city in the early 20th century, defining new urban axes and stimulating the development of new housing districts. The project proposal aims to fully integrate the area of the Ex Marcello – Ex Gas in the rest of the city, improving the functional and spatial relations with the nearby sites, the adjacent structures and the sports centre, as well as the living conditions and collective well-being, establishing a feeling of renewed identity and a sense of belonging to the places.

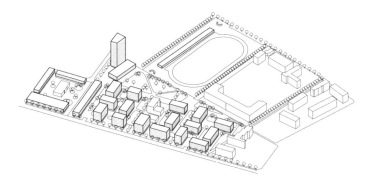

100

SENIORENRESIDENZ, BALERNA
Wettbewerb 2019, 1. Preis

Das Neubauprojekt manifestiert den respektvollen Umgang mit der bestehenden Seniorenresidenz und dem Umfeld der angrenzenden historischen Bauten. Der zentrale Innenhof, der durch das neue Volumen definiert ist, versorgt die Haupträume der Anlage mit Licht und gewährleistet innen die gewünschte räumliche Qualität. Im städtischen Massstab lässt sich die Grösse des Innenhofs als «Freiraum» auffassen. Die architektonische Formensprache und die formale Komposition des Gebäudes zeichnen sich durch eine Materialität aus, die respektvoll auf den Kontext eingeht, sodass sich das Gebäude harmonisch in die umliegende Landschaft einfügt.

SENIORS CITIZENS' RESIDENCE, BALERNA
Competition 2019, 1st Prize

The project is characterised by the coordinated insertion of a new building both with respect to the existing senior citizens' residence complex and the context of the adjacent historical fabric. The central courtyard, which is defined by the new volume, supplies the main spaces of the complex with light, guaranteeing the desired interior spatial quality. On an urban scale, the patio dimensions allow it to be perceived as a "void". The architectural language and formal composition of the building is characterised by a materiality that respects the context, while allowing it to integrate harmoniously into the surrounding landscape.

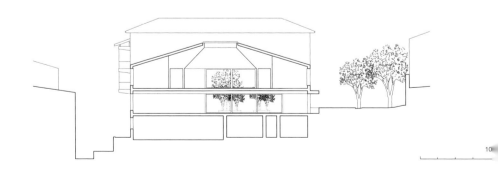

10

MATTEO INCHES

1984	geboren in Brescia (IT)
1985	Umzug nach Vacallo
2003–2009	Studium der Architektur an der AAM, Accademia di Architettura in Mendrisio
2005–2006	Trainee bei JMA Architects, Brisbane (AU)
2009–2011	Architekt bei Buzzi e Buzzi architetti, Locarno
2011–2013	Projektassistent an der USI, Accademia di Architettura di Mendrisio
2010–2017	Inhaber des Studio inches architettura
2017–	Mitinhaber bei Inches Geleta Architetti Sagl, Locarno
2018–	Mitglied bei BSA/FAS, Bund Schweizer Architekten
2019–	Vorstandsmitglied bei BSA/FAS, Ortsgruppe Tessin

NASTASJA INCHES-GELETA

1984	geboren in Rheine (DE)
2009	Umzug nach Vacallo
2011–2014	Studium der Innenarchitektur an der SUPSI, Scuola universitaria professionale della Svizzera italiana, Lugano
2014	Zusammenarbeit mit Matteo Inches im Studio inches architettura
2015	Vorstandsmitglied bei VSI/ASAI, Ortsgruppe Tessin
2015–2016	Projektassistentin an der SUPSI, Scuola universitaria professionale della Svizzera italiana, Lugano
2017–	Mitinhaberin bei Inches Geleta Architetti Sagl, Locarno

MITARBEITENDE (aktuell*)	Tommaso Fantini, Perica Kovac, Giovanni Lazzareschi, Matteo Lorenzini, Marta Mascheroni*, Tommaso Pareschi, Alberto Rossi, Luca Suriano, Emilio Trevisiol, Marija Urbaite

MATTEO INCHES

1984	Born in Brescia (IT)
1985	Moved to Switzerland (Vacallo)
2003–2009	Studied Architecture at the AAM, Accademia di Architettura, Mendrisio
2005–2006	Trainee architect at JMA Architects, Brisbane (AU)
2009–2011	Architect at Buzzi e Buzzi architetti, Locarno
2011–2013	Project Assistant at USI, Accademia di Architettura, Mendrisio
2010–2017	Owner of the studio inches architettura
2017–	Partner at Inches Geleta Architetti Sagl, Locarno
2018–	BSA/FAS member, Federation of Swiss Architects
2019–	BSA/FAS Board Member, Ticino section

NASTASJA INCHES-GELETA

1984	Born in Rheine (DE)
2009	Moved to Switzerland (Vacallo)
2011–2014	Studied Interior Architecture at the SUPSI, Lugano
2014	Joined Matteo Inches at studio inches architettura VSI/ASAI Board Member, Ticino section
2015–2016	Project Assistant at SUPSI, Lugano
2017–	Partner at Inches Geleta Architetti Sagl, Locarno

Collaborators (current*)	Tommaso Fantini, Perica Kovac, Giovanni Lazzareschi, Matteo Lorenzini, Marta Mascheroni*, Tommaso Pareschi, Alberto Rossi, Luca Suriano, Emilio Trevisiol, Marija Urbaite

WERKVERZEICHNIS

2011	Wettbewerb, Schulerweiterung, Savosa, 3. Preis
2012	Haus Rizza, Vacallo
2013	Wettbewerb, CECAL, Kantonale Einsatzzentrale, Bellinzona, 4. Preis
2014	Museum MeCrì, Minusio
	Häuser Moccetti und Bedano, Projekt
	Wettbewerb, Pfarrzentrum, Giubiasco, 6. Preis; in Zusammenarbeit mit dem Architekten Roberto Briccola
2015	Haus Desgraz, Solduno
	Wohnhaus Infinity, Locarno, Projekt
	Möbel Mastrillo-Rossi, Bellinzona
	Wettbewerb, Erweiterung Seniorenresidenz, Losone, 6. Preis; in Zusammenarbeit mit dem Buzzi studio d'architettura
2016	Pavillon MeCrì, Minusio
	Haus Pallone, Claro, Projekt
	Wohngebäude La Santa, Lugano, Projekt
	Wettbewerb, Erweiterung Krankenhaus EOC, Lugano, 3. Preis; in Zusammenarbeit mit Baumschlager Eberle Architekten, St. Gallen
2017	Wohnung Speziali, Locarno
	Haus Facchini, Giubiasco, Projekt
	privater Wettbewerb, Wohnhäuser auf einem Hügel, Orselina
	beschränkter Wettbewerb, Erweiterung Krankenhaus, Bellinzona; in Zusammenarbeit mit Baumschlager Eberle Architekten, St. Gallen
	Wettbewerb, Schulerweiterung, Lugano, 1. Preis
2018	Palazzo Pioda, Locarno
	Wettbewerb, Schulerweiterung, Melano, 1. Preis
	Masterplan Ex Macello – Ex Gas, Locarno, 1. Preis
2019	Piazza San Simone, Vacallo
	Wettbewerb, Seniorenresidenz, Balerna, 1. Preis; in Zusammenarbeit mit Baumschlager Eberle Architekten, St. Gallen
2020–	Kulturzentrum Elisarion, Minusio
	Haus Weidmann, Maggia

AUSZEICHNUNGEN

2014	A+ Award 2014, Finalist für Haus Rizza
2016	Der Beste Umbau, Finalist für Haus Rizza
2017	A+ Award 2017, Auszeichnung für Pavillon MeCrì
	Swiss Art Award 2017, Finalist
2018	best architect 18, Award für Pavillon MeCrì
2019	best architect 19, Award für Palazzo Pioda

AUSSTELLUNGEN

2016	«Architektur0.16», MAAG Halle, Zürich
2017	«Schweizweit», S AM Schweizerisches Architektur-museum, Basel
	«Swiss Art Award 2017», Messe Basel, Halle 3, Basel
	«Schweizweit», Architettura recente in Svizzera, Lugano

LIST OF WORKS

2011	Competition, school extension, Savosa, 3rd Prize
2012	Rizza House, Vacallo
2013	Competition, public safety headquarters, Bellinzona, 1st Purchase
2014	MeCrì Museum, Minusio
	Moccetti Houses, Bedano, project
	Competition, parrish centre, Giubiasco, 6th Prize; in collaboration with arch. Roberto Briccola
2015	Desgraz House, Solduno
	Infinity residence, Locarno, project
	Mastrillo-Rossi furniture, Bellinzona
	Competition, senior citizens' residence extension, Losone, 6th Prize; in collaboration with Buzzi studio d'architettura
2016	MeCrì Pavilion, Minusio
	Pallone House, Claro, project
	La Santa residential building, Lugano, project
	Competition, EOC Hospital extension, Lugano, 3rd Prize; in collaboration with Baumschlager Eberle Architekten, St Gallen
2017	Speziali apartment, Locarno
	Facchini House, Giubiasco, project
	Private competition, residences on a slope, Orselina
	Restricted competition, hospital extension, Bellinzona; in collaboration with Baumschlager Eberle Architekten, St Gallen
	Competition, school extension, Lugano, 1st Prize
2018	Palazzo Pioda, Locarno
	Competition, school extension, Melano, 1st Prize
	Masterplan Ex Macello – Ex Gas, Locarno, 1st Prize
2019	S. Simone public square, Vacallo
	Competition, senior citizens' residence extension, Balerna, 1st Prize; in collaboration with Baumschlager Eberle Architekten, St Gallen
2020–	Elisarion cultural centre, Minusio
	Weidmann House, Maggia

AWARDS

2014	A+ Award 2014, finalist. Rizza House
2016	Der Beste Umbau, finalist. Rizza House
2017	A+ Award 2017, distinction. MeCrì Pavilion
	Swiss Art Award 2017, finalist
2018	"best architect 18" Award. MeCrì Pavilion
2019	"best architect 19" Award. Palazzo Pioda

EXHIBITIONS

2016	"Architektur0.16". Maag Halle, Zurich
2017	"Schweizweit". S AM Architecture Museum Basel, Basel
	"Swiss Art Award 2017". Messe Basel, Hall 3, Basel
	"Schweizweit". Architettura recente in Svizzera, Lugano

VORLESUNGEN/KONFERENZEN

2016	«Trasformazioni», Accademia di architettura di Mendrisio. Atelier Canevascini
2017	«Continuum», Politecnico di Milano. Lab. Prof. Scaramellini
2018	«Inches Geleta», Nomad Hotel, Warm-up Open House Basel 2018, Basel
2019	«Das Bild als Referenz», Swisness Applied Exhibition, Kunsthaus Glarus
	«Inches Geleta», Fakultät für Architektur, Technische Universität München (DE)
	«Inches Geleta», Politecnico di Milano, sede Piacenza, Lab. Prof. Ghilotti

BIBLIOGRAFIE

2013	C3, Nr. 338. «Urban How. Constraints to Blessings», Seoul (KR)
2014	Mark, Nr. 51. Notice Board. Frame Publishers, Amsterdam (NL)
2015	Umbauen + Renovieren, Nr. 4/15. «Neues Innenleben», Architema Verlag, Zürich
2016	Archi, Nr. 1/16. «Spazi per l'arte in Ticino», Zürich
	Der beste Umbau Architekturpreis 16, Architema Verlag, Zürich
	TEC21, Nr. 47, «Baujuwelen im Goldregen», Espazium Verlag, Zürich
2017	«best architects 18 Award», zinnobergruen, Düsseldorf (DE)
	Modulør, Nr. 3/17 «Steinerne Schweiz», NZZ Fachmedien, Urdorf
2018	as, Nr. 209 Architecture Suisse, Verlag, Hrsg. Frederic Krafft-Gloria, Pully
	Faces, Nr. 74 «GranTicino», Hrsg. Infolio, Gollion
	«best architects 19 Award», zinnobergruen, Düsseldorf (DE)
2019	a + u, Nr. 580 «Re: Swiss – Emerging Architects Under 45 in Switzerland», Shinkenchiku-sha Co. Ltd (JP)
	Archi, Nr. 2/19, «L'eredità dell'Accademia in Ticino», Espazium, Zürich

LECTURES/CONFERENCES

2016	"Trasformazioni". Accademia di architettura di Mendrisio. Atelier Canevascini 2019
2017	"Continuum". Politecnico di Milano. Lab. prof. Scaramellini
2018	"Inches Geleta". Nomad Hotel. WarmUp-Open House Basel 2018, Basel
2019	"Das Bild als Referenz". Swisness Applied Exhibition. Kunsthaus Glarus
	"Inches Geleta". Faculty of Architecture. Technische Universität München
	"Inches Geleta". Politecnico di Milano, sede Piacenza. Lab. prof. Ghilotti

BIBLIOGRAPHY

2013	*C3*. N°338. "Urban How. Constraints to Blessings". Seul (KP)
2014	*Mark*. N°51. Notice Board. Frame Publishers. Amsterdam (NL)
2015	*Umbauen+Renovieren*. N°4/15. "Neues Innenleben". Architema Verlag, Zurich
2016	*Archi*. N°1/16 . "Spazi per l'arte in Ticino". Espazium, Zurich
	Der beste Umbau Architekturpreis 16. Architema Verlag, Zurich
	TEC21. N°47. "Baujuwelen im Goldregen". Espazium Verlag, Zurich
2017	*"best architects 18 Award" Book*. zinnobergruen, Düsseldorf (DE)
	Modulør. N°3/17 "Steinerne Schweiz". NZZ Fachmedien, Urdorf
2018	*as*. N°209 Architecture Suisse. Verlag – Frederic Krafft-Gloria (Ed.), Pully
	Faces. N°74 "GranTicino". Ed. Infolio, Gollion
	"best architects 19 Award" Book. zinnobergruen, Düsseldorf (DE)
2019	*a+u*. N°580 "Re: Swiss – Emerging Architects Under 45 in Switzerland". Shinkenchiku-sha Co. Ltd (JP)
	Archi. N°2/19. "L'eredità dell'Accademia in Ticino". Espazium, Zurich

Finanzielle und ideelle Unterstützung

Ein besonderer Dank gilt den Institutionen und Sponsorfirmen, deren finanzielle Unterstützungen wesentlich zum Erscheinen dieser Buchreihe beitragen. Ihr kulturelles Engagement ermöglicht ein fruchtbares und freundschaftliches Zusammenwirken von Baukultur und Bauwirtschaft.

Financial and conceptual support

Special thanks to the institutions and sponsoring companies whose financial support makes a key contribution to the production of this book series. Their cultural engagement encourages fruitful, friendly interaction between building culture and the building industry.

Schweizerische Eidgenossenschaft
Confédération suisse
Confederazione Svizzera
Confederaziun svizra

Eidgenössisches Departement des Innern EDI
Bundesamt für Kultur BAK

Scuola universitaria professionale
della Svizzera italiana

B&L Laudato SA, Ligornetto

Cocoon System AG, Basel

DECO Coppolino SA, Minusio

Desax AG, Gommiswald

EcoControl SA, Locarno/Lugano

ETAVIS Elettro-Impianti SA, Locarno

Fondazione Museo Mecrì, Minusio

Forbo-Giubiasco SA, Giubiasco

Gamboni – Salmina SA, Gordola

JELMONI
INGEGNERIA SA
JELMONI-SA.CH

Jelmoni Ingegneria SA, Ascona

Montana Sistemi di Costruzione SA, Villmergen

Scherler SA, Lugano-Breganzona

Visani Rusconi Talleri SA, Taverne/Losone

veragouth xilema

Veragouth SA, Bedano

V-ZUG SA, Bellinzona